THE GRECO-ROMAN BOOK
WARFARE BY DUCT TAPE

DISCLAIMER AND TERMS OF USE AGREEMENT

The author and publisher of this ebook and the accompanying materials have used their best efforts in preparing this ebook. The author and publisher make no representation or warranties with respect to the accuracy, applicability, fitness, or completeness of the contents of this ebook. The information contained in this ebook is strictly for educational purposes. Therefore, if you wish to apply ideas contained in this ebook, you are taking full responsibility for your actions.

The author and publisher disclaim any warranties (express or implied), merchantability, or fitness for any particular purpose. The author and publisher shall in no event be held liable to any party for any direct, indirect, punitive, special, incidental or other consequential damages arising directly or indirectly from any use of this material, which is provided "as is", and without warranties.

As always, the advice of a competent legal, tax, accounting or other professional should be sought.

ISBN-13: 978-1-942006-06-0

TABLE OF CONTENTS

"Had I sons I should train them as your husband intends to train your son. It may be that he will never be called upon to draw a sword, but the time he has spent in acquiring its use will not be wasted. These exercises give firmness and suppleness to the figure, quickness to the eye, and briskness of decision to the mind. A man who knows that he can at need defend his life if attacked, whether against soldiers in the field or robbers in the street, has a sense of power and self-reliance that a man untrained in the use of the strength God has given him can never feel. I was instructed in arms when a boy, and I am none the worse for it."
- G. A. Henty
St. Bartholomew's Eve

THE WEAPONS

These weapons were chosen because they were used primarily by the Greco-Roman people in their expansions around the world.

THE SPEAR = HASTA

The spear was used by the Greeks and the Romans, although the Greeks were much more widely known for using it. Originally, the spear used by the Greeks would have been nine feet long, but we decided to shorten ours up for modern convenience. The Greeks would line up in dense phalanx formations with spears facing outwards. This worked well in a head-on fight, but it was bad for maneuvering, and use on rough terrain.

The Romans used spears in certain campaigns in certain cohorts. On Tarjan's column, in Rome, there are carved pictures of legionaries using hastas, which were about seven feet long, against their enemies, the Dacians.

THE BASIC SWORD = XIPHOS

The Greeks used a straight, double-edged iron sword. It was heavier at the point of the blade, which made it a little easier for swinging at enemies and had more momentum during the strike than other swords. The Greeks only used their swords when their spears had been broken in a fight.

The Romans used the basic sword only during the end of the empire, while imitating the Barbarian style of fighting.

THE SHORT SWORD = GLADIUS

The Romans originally learned about the short sword while fighting Iberian mercenaries in the first Punic war. They saw its deadly effectiveness in close quarters. They made it the standard hand-to-hand weapon soon after. It's good for fighting in close quarters and when there are people standing behind you – it does not take much room to swing. It was a short, about fifteen inches long, double-edged iron (and later steel) sword.

THE JAVELIN = PILUM

The javelin was a basic missile hurled at enemies from a distance. The Greek javelin had a basic wooden shaft with a sharp iron head.

The Roman javelin, or Pilum, (plural, Pila) had a long, soft iron head which, when it hit the enemy, would hopefully pierce through the shield and hit the person behind. Or, it would stick in the shield, then bend, making the shield exceedingly heavy, weighing it down and making it practically useless. If it hit the ground it would also bend, and could not be thrown back – a useful feature in warfare!

DAGGER = PUGIO

The Roman dagger, or Pugio, was double-edged, made out of iron or steel, and worn in the belt as a tool, and possibly weapon. It was shorter than the short sword, about the length of a modern knife. The Roman version would probably not have much decoration. Decoration of daggers was not done until the early medieval ages.

SHIELDS = SCUTUM

The Greek shield was perfectly round, slightly domed, made of wood, leather, and bronze. It weighed about fifteen pounds and was approximately four feet in diameter. The outside was plated with bronze, and sometimes had an emblem painted on it. Some Greek warriors of the Seleucid Empire had their shields plated with silver on the outside. They formed a large cohort called the Silver Band.

The Roman shield, or Scutum, was made of wood covered with painted leather and had an iron boss in the center, which was part of the handle. It was rather large, large enough to protect most of a legionary, rectangularly shaped with a slight outward-facing convex curve.

HELMETS = GALEA

We have two styles of helmets in this book. One, a Greek-style design is based off the Corinthian type of helmet, which was common in the 5th century B. C. This helmet was made from bronze and provided good protection, although it was hard to see and hear while wearing it.

The other design is based off of the Roman Coolus type from the first century A. D. It was made of bronze and later iron. It was distinctive from the Greek style in that it had a large neck-guard at the back (not included) and sometimes had a small spike at the top. It did not have a nose-guard. The Roman officer would often have a crest on top of his helmet, while the common soldier did not. With the Greeks, everybody had a crest.

DESCRIPTION OF THE BATTLE GAME

Battling is at least two teams fighting each other using weapons. We suggest using our foam weapons to minimize injuries.

Divide your players into two teams of about the same strength and even numbers. Say there are four big guys and four little guys. There should be two big guys and two little guys on each team.

Weather is no deterrent to battling. We have had battles in rain and heat.

Object of the game: divide and conquer your enemy!

More than one battle can be played. It is important to keep score of who wins each battle. The one who wins the most battles is the victor!

You can use fortifications. Tree houses work well. Piles of logs or even swing sets can be used.

Naval battles can be fought using non-motor boats such as canoes and row boats. To fight a naval battle, simply row up to them and fight them. Do not use throwing axes, they are not waterproof.

With fortifications, it is often wise to use your spear instead of your axe or sword. The spear has greater length which is helpful in forts. It is very wise to use missiles (water balloons, throwing axes, etc.) so you can bombard the enemy without having to storm the gate.

It is crucial to use shields. People who do not use shields are usually slain early in the battle and are vulnerable to throwing axes and heavy weapons such as battle axes.

Terrible war cries intimidate the enemy.

It is important to have one main leader (general). This keeps the army unified and reduces squabbles.

RULES OF THE BATTLE GAME

RULE #1
Chivalry and honor must be exhibited at all times.

RULE #2
If any weapon hits your limb (for ex. arm, leg, hand), you are no longer able to use it. If you are holding a weapon in the hand or arm that is hit, you can't keep using the weapon with **that** arm but could switch it to the other arm and keep fighting. If both arms are hit, you must surrender or run away.
If your leg is hit, you must limp. If both legs are hit, you must kneel or squat.
If you lose all your limbs, you are doomed!

RULE #3
If you get hit in the head, neck or torso, you are officially dead and can't play until the end of the battle.

RULE #4
The only way to win a battle is when all of the enemy (other team) is dead, has surrendered or has run away (escaped).
If a team holding prisoners is defeated, the prisoners are automatically freed.

RULE #5
If someone surrenders, you can either keep them captive, (they are not allowed to escape) or release them and they are free to return to their army (team).

RULE #6
Parley~ A parley is when one or possibly two people from each team talk to each other. To start a parley, one team member must say, "I request an audience." If the other team agrees, they send a person forward to talk to the other.
It is usually used for discussing the release of prisoners by ransom or switching of players. You can be chivalrous and release prisoners. It is important to not carry weapons but must leave them behind during a parley to avoid treachery.

RULE #7
We believe that only boys should battle with other boys. Young men should practice protecting young ladies so it is not appropriate to fight them.

RULE #8
Ransom~A ransom is when a soldier who is captured is released by a payment of money. You can make your own money by folding tin foil into circles, the shape of coins. To ransom a prisoner, first call a parley and then negotiate the price. A general usually costs more than the average soldier. (This rule is optional.)

WEAPON INSTRUCTIONS

PVC pipe tips: You can find PVC pipe at your local hardware store like Lowe's and Home Depot. You will need a pipe cutter or a saw to cut the PVC pipe to the correct length. If you do not have a saw, the large hardware stores will usually cut it for you.

PVC pipe insulation~the black foam stuff. We usually buy this at the same stores as the PVC pipe. We like the kind that comes in a 4 pack of 3 foot pieces. It says on the package that it is for copper pipe but it works just fine for these weapons.

Foam~the 2 inch thick green stuff. You can find this foam at Wal-Mart and fabric stores like JoAnn.com and Hobby Lobby. It comes in small packages or in large pieces by the yard.

Cardboard: It can be difficult to cut cardboard so younger kids might need some help or supervision. In most of the pieces that use cardboard, it is important to cut the cardboard so the "ridges" (inner corrugated sections) **run across** the narrow width of the piece. This way the piece can bend properly. Check instructions before tracing the pattern onto the cardboard.

½ Width Piece of Duct Tape: Before we begin the weapon instructions, we need to define a term we will use in the book: "½ width". To make a ½ width piece of duct tape, take a piece of duct tape and tear it lengthwise (the long way). Now you have two ½ width pieces of duct tape. Sometimes, even a ¼ width piece of duct tape is used. Just tear the ½ width piece again to make the ¼ width.

Now, on to the fun!

SWORD~
~XIPHOS~

Materials:
3 foot piece of ¾ inch PVC pipe
3 foot piece of PVC pipe insulation
(We use 3/8" thick polyethylene foam, fits ¾" pipe)
Duct tape
Scissors
(You may need a saw to cut the PVC to size)
   Please Note: This project may require adult help to use the sharp tools.

Directions:
Cut 8 inches off of your 3 foot piece of insulation.

Next, take the larger piece of insulation and slide it down the 3-foot PVC pipe.

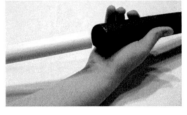

Leave about 1 inch extending off of the PVC at the point of the sword.

Take the 8 inch piece of insulation foam.
There is a seam down the length of it. Cut a slit 2 inches long on the seam in the middle (center) of the piece.
On the opposite side from the seam cut another slit.

Slide the piece of foam onto the PVC pipe to form the hilt of the sword.

Crisscross the duct tape around the hilt to strengthen it.

Tape across the end of the hilt, turn and do it again. Then tape around the end to make it smooth.
Do this on both ends of the hilt.

Cover the entire hilt with duct tape.
Be sure to wrap around the pipe/ handle.

Tape the point (end) of the sword blade the same way. Wrap the duct tape around a few times to strengthen it so it won't tear during battle.

Now tape the blade. It is helpful to have another person. Start at the hilt and wrap on a slightly diagonal angle towards the tip of the blade.

Cover the handle. Cap the end just as you did with the end of the blade.

Decorate as desired. Often wealthy Greeks and Romans would put a jewel in the center of the hilt.

SHORT SWORD~
~GLADIUS~

Materials:

2 foot piece of ¾ inch PVC pipe
2 foot piece of PVC pipe insulation
(We use 3/8" thick polyethylene foam, fits ¾" pipe)
Duct tape
Scissors
(You may need a saw to cut the PVC to size)

      Please Note: This project may require adult help to use the sharp tools.

Directions:
Cut 5 inches off of your 2 foot piece of insulation. Follow the directions for the long sword (except you have a 5 inch piece of insulation instead of 8 inch). The rest is the same as the long sword.

SPEAR~
~HASTA~

Materials:
4 foot piece of ¾ inch PVC pipe
1 foot piece of PVC pipe insulation
(We use 3/8" thick polyethylene foam, fits ¾" pipe)
Duct tape
Scissors
(You may need a saw to cut the PVC to size)

      Please Note: This project may require adult help to use the sharp tools.

Directions:
Slide the 1 foot piece of pipe insulation onto the PVC pipe. Leave at least 2 inches extending past the end of the PVC pipe.

Tape across the end of the insulation at the tip of the spear, turn and repeat. Then tape around the end to make it smooth.

Starting at the tip, wrap the duct tape on a slightly diagonal angle until the insulation is covered and just onto the PVC pipe.

Tape around the base of the blade over the PVC pipe to reinforce it.

Then, taking the color of your choice, tape a long strip down the length of the pipe. Smooth edges of tape.

Tuck end of the tape into the open end of the PVC pipe.

Repeat on the reverse side of the PVC pipe so that the handle is covered. It usually takes 2 strips of duct tape to cover the handle of the spear.

Decorate as desired.

DAGGER~
~PUGIO~

Materials:

6 inch piece of ¾ inch PVC pipe
8 inch piece of PVC pipe insulation
(We use 3/8" thick polyethylene foam, fits ¾"
pipe)
Duct tape
Scissors
(You may need a saw to cut the PVC to size)

Please Note: This project may require adult help to use the sharp tools.

Directions:

Slide the insulation onto the PVC pipe
leaving 4 inches for the handle.

Tape across the end of the insulation at
the tip of the spear, turn and repeat.
Then tape around the end to make it
smooth.

Starting at the tip, wrap the duct tape on a
slightly diagonal angle until the insulation
is covered and just onto the PVC pipe.

Tape around the base of the blade over the PVC pipe to
reinforce it.
Cover handle with the color of your choice, tucking in the ends
as you go. Decorate as desired.

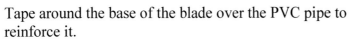

JAVELIN~
~PILUM~

Materials:
4 foot dowel, 5/16 inch diameter
2 plastic grocery bags
Duct tape
Scissors

Directions:
Squish bags into shape of a teardrop (oval with a point at the end). Place over the end of the dowel.

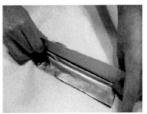

Wrap duct tape over the bags to form a teardrop (oval with a point at the end).

Cover all of the bags making sure to get the tape on the dowel below the bags.

Place the long edge of a piece of duct tape at the end of the dowel to form a frill (fletching). Place another piece of duct tape on the first, sticky sides together.

Repeat to form 3 sections of the frill. See pictures.

Trim on the diagonal at the upper part of the frill.
Please note: This javelin should only be used to throw at targets, not in a game of battle. It not safe for throwing at people! Use at your own risk.

JAVELIN (FOAM) ~
~PILUM~

Materials:
5 inch piece of ¾ inch PVC pipe
2 feet 7 inches piece of PVC pipe insulation
(we'll call it foam)
Duct tape
Scissors
(You may need a saw to cut the PVC to size)
　　　Please Note: This project may
require adult help to use the sharp tools.

Directions:
Slide the PVC pipe into the foam
until it is about 3 inches **in** from
the end. (It is the weight to keep
the javelin flying straight.)
It should not be visible past the
foam.

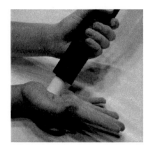

Cap the end by putting duct tape over the end, turn and
repeat.

Tape around the end.

Tape around the foam where the piece of PVC pipe is to keep the foam from splitting.

To make the frill, cut a piece of duct tape 6 inches long. Place on
foam long-ways but only press down half of the width of the tape.

Lay the next piece about 1 inch from the first piece. Press onto the foam and then pinch together with the first piece so that it stands up.

Do this 2 more times to make 3 frills. Position the duct tape so that the frills are on 3 opposite sides, like N, SE and SW on the compass, as shown below.

Trim the top of the frills on the diagonal.

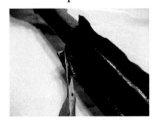

This javelin is much safer than the wooden one and we use it in battling. But use it at your own risk.

SHIELD~
~SCUTUM~

Materials:
Plywood, size and shape of your choice
Four (4) small blocks of wood 3 ½" x 1 ½" x ½"
Cardboard
Duct Tape
Four (4) Screws 1 ½" long (or long enough to go through the blocks of wood, cardboard and plywood)
Saw (to cut plywood if needed)
Screwdriver
Sandpaper
Scissors

       Please Note: This project may require adult help to use the sharp tools.

Directions:
Before you begin cutting the wood, plan how big you want your shield to be. We recommend you measure your arm from the elbow to the knuckles on your hand when you make a fist. The shield should be at least this wide.

Take a piece of plywood and cut to the shape (square, circle, oval, or rectangle) you want for the shield. Either sand the wood or cover the front with duct tape. You may want to add details with duct tape. Usually, we cover the front of the shield with duct tape and sand the back well so that we don't get splinters.

Cut a strip of cardboard 18" long by 4" wide. Cover with duct tape so as to strengthen it. Cut another strip of cardboard 12" long by 2" wide. Also cover with duct tape.

Bend up 1 inch on the ends and curve the rest of the piece of cardboard. Do this to both pieces.

Measure where the large piece of cardboard should go using your arm. Place it near your elbow. (You may need a friend to help you with this.)

Tape down the ends.

Place a block of wood on the end and screw down on each end of the block. Do this on both ends of the piece.
If you have a power screw driver you may want to pre-drill the holes. You can use a regular screwdriver also.

Measure where the smaller piece should go by placing your arm in the large piece. You will grip the smaller piece so place accordingly.

Tape ends to hold in place. Place a block of wood on the end and screw down on each end of the block. Do this on both ends of the piece.

It should look something like this when it is finished.

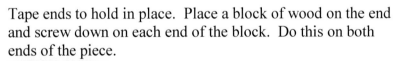

The shield is done. Decorate as you desire.

GREEK HELMET~
~GALEA~

Materials:
Patterns
Cardstock
Cardboard
Duct Tape
Scissors
Clear "scotch" tape

Directions:

Before we begin, we need to explain that there are two ways to make the back of the helmets. The first way will be shown with the Greek helmet and the other will be shown with the Roman helmet. Either way will work with both helmets.

Print the helmet pieces on cardstock and cut them out. (If you want the helmet in a smaller size, try minimizing the patterns on a copy machine.) Tape together the upper helmet pieces at the center front with the "scotch" tape.

Tape together the other edges at the top of the helmet pieces.

Tape lower pieces to upper pieces matching the overlap dotted lines.

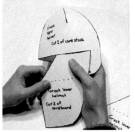 

Cut a small piece of cardboard (about 1" x 3") for the nose piece. Cover it in duct tape.

Try on helmet, center the nose piece and then tape it on to the center front.

To strengthen the sides, cut

cardboard to fit and tape in place.

Cover entire helmet in duct tape.

To make the back of the helmet: Cut the back helmet piece out of cardboard and cover it in duct tape. Cut another piece of cardboard long enough to go all the way across the back of your head and 2 inches wide. Tape it to the crosspiece at the bottom of the back helmet piece. Cover it in duct tape. Tape the top of the back helmet piece to the top of the helmet.

Try on the helmet then tape the ends to the sides to make a firm back to the helmet as shown in the picture. (This is the first option for the back of the helmet. See the Roman helmet for the other option.)

This is what you have so far.

To make the crest: Cut 1 crest piece from cardboard. Cut 2 small rectangles about 1" x 3". Bend them in half to form an L (90° angle). Tape to the back of the helmet just a little past the top so they are standing up.

Put the crest piece between the small cardboard pieces and tape. The crest can be touching the helmet or be just above it.

Cover the crest with duct tape. Use a different color if you prefer.

Attach front point of the crest to the front of the helmet.
We recommend that the inside of the helmet be covered in duct tape also. It helps it last longer.

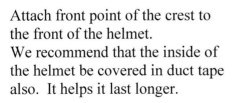

ROMAN HELMET~
~GALEA~

Materials:

Patterns

Duct Tape~<small>Shiny silver looks better than the gray but it is optional.</small>

Cardstock

Cardboard

Elastic~<small>about ¾" wide by about 8 inches long (If you choose this option, see instructions)</small>

Stapler/Staples

Clear "scotch" tape and Scissors

Directions:

Before we begin, we need to explain that there are two ways to make the back of the helmets. The first way will be shown with the Greek helmet and the other will be shown with the Roman helmet. Either way will work with both helmets.

Print the helmet pieces on cardstock and cut them out. (If you want the helmet in a smaller size, try minimizing the patterns on a copy machine.) Tape together the upper helmet pieces at the center front with the "scotch" tape.

Tape together the other edges at the top of the helmet pieces.
Cut the lower helmet pieces out of cardboard.
Tape lower pieces to upper pieces matching the overlap dotted lines. Check that the pieces are even with each other.

Cover lower half with duct tape.

Place a piece of duct tape across the front, right above the eye hole.

Cover the upper helmet with duct tape.

Front forehead piece: Cut a piece of cardboard 7 ½" x 3". Bend in half. Cut off a narrow triangle, starting at the 3" end and angling toward the center.

Cover with duct tape.

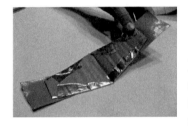

Put tape on each small end and tape the forehead piece above eye hole across the brow.
Cover the inside of the helmet with duct tape.

Cut the back helmet piece out of cardboard. Cover completely with duct tape. Bend it to make it curved to fit your head. Tape it to the top of the helmet.

Cut the elastic in half making two (2) pieces.

Staple the elastic to the back helmet piece. Make sure the "pokey" part of the staple is on the outside so it doesn't catch your hair. Try on the helmet and fit the elastic to the sides and staple in place.

You're done. Good job!!

COSTUMES

TUNIC~
~TUNICA~

Materials:
Some sort of fabric-knit, sheets, curtains, or whatever you have
Belt or material for a sash
Scissors
Sewing machine or needle and thread

Directions:
First determine the size you will need. Most tunics in the Greek and Roman time went down to the knees and had no sleeves. They draped over the shoulders a little bit. The size of your fabric may determine the width or measure across the shoulders. Make it wide enough so that you can slip it over your head and shoulders and get the arms out of the arm holes. If you have enough fabric, double the length so you won't need to sew a seam across the shoulders.

Cut a hole for the head to go through. The No-Sew Option is to just pull the tunic over the head and use a belt to keep it around the waist.

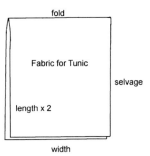

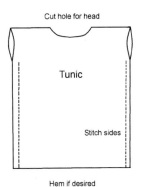

The sewing option is to sew up the sides but leave an arm hole. Hem the bottom if desired. Knit fabric is nice because it doesn't fray and you won't have to hem the edges.

In the early Roman times, soldiers only wore sleeveless tunics. It was considered too feminine to have sleeves. But near the end of the Roman era, it was acceptable to wear sleeves.

If you want sleeves in your tunic, make a "T" shape of fabric and then sew up the sides. Be sure the main body of the tunic is wide enough so that you can get it on and get the arms through the sleeves. Maybe almost double the width across the front of the person.

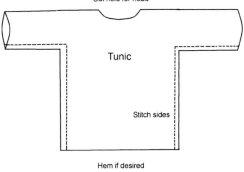

Some children are small and the hole in the neck will gap too much. Just add a button and loop at the back of the neck to close it a little. See Cloak instructions.

Use a belt or cut a strip of fabric to wrap around the waist. The tunic was considered underclothing that was worn under armor or a toga.

CLOAK~
~ABOLLA~

Materials:
Some sort of fabric-knit, sheets, curtains, or whatever you have
Button
Thin piece of elastic, ribbon, or string
Couple of pins
Scissors
Needle and thread

Directions:
Determine the size of cape that you need. Do you want a cloak that goes down to the knees or almost to the floor? That is your length measurement plus an inch to turn over at the neck. The width of your fabric may determine your width of the cloak, otherwise decide how wide you want it.

Cut your fabric to size. If you are using a fabric that will fray, you may want to hem the sides first. Fold over an inch the top edge which will go by the neck. Try it on. Clasp the cape closed a few inches down from the front of the neck. This where you will attach the button and elastic (ribbon). Mark it on both sides with a pin. Sew on the button on one side. Measure a small piece of elastic (ribbon) around the button so you can still get it on and off. Stitch elastic (ribbon) on both ends to the cape at the mark.

Throw over the shoulders and button at the neck.

~BRACAE OR BRACCAE~
The Romans wore pants under their tunics in cooler weather, so if you wear pants under your tunic you will still be authentic.

MONEY POUCH~

Materials:
Fabric: see instructions
String, rope, ribbon, shoe lace or whatever you have
Safety pin
Scissors
Sewing machine or needle and thread
Option: Leg from a pair of cut off pants

Directions:

You can make a money pouch out of almost anything. If you want a money pouch that is a bit fancier, you can use fabric. We just happened to have a scrap of velour that we used for a pouch. Knit fabric won't fray and is easier but any durable fabric will work.

Determine the size of pouch that you want. For example, if you want a pouch that is 5" x 7", allowing for seam allowances and the casing for the drawstring, cut two (2) squares of 6" x 8 ½". You can also cut a long rectangle and just fold over so that you eliminate one seam. The rectangle would be 6" x 16".

Put the right sides together and sew up the seams leaving one 6" side open (use ½" seam). Turn over 1" at the opening. Stitch around using a small seam of about ¼". On the side or center front, make a small cut in the casing only on the front piece big enough for the drawstring to go through.

Cut your drawstring to at least twice the length of your opening. In this example, the opening is 10" after sewing, so the drawstring should be 20" long. Put the safety pin in the end of the drawstring and push it through the casing.

A leg from a pair of pants that was cut off into shorts can be made into a pouch. Cut to the size you want. Sew one end. Cut small slits about an inch apart and weave your drawstring in and out through the slits. If you don't have any, thrift stores and yard sales often have pants for cheap.

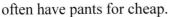

COIN MONEY FOR RANSOM~

Materials:
Aluminum foil
Something heavy like a hammer or shoe

Directions:
Take a small piece of aluminum foil about twice the size you want the coin to be and fold in the edges to make a circle. It's all right if it is not perfectly round, ancient money wasn't perfect either. Press down firmly against a hard surface and then hammer flat with the heel of a shoe or a hammer.

Mark the coins with designs or figures so you know which coins belong to you. You can also make a money pouch to keep your money in while you are battling. See instructions for money pouch.

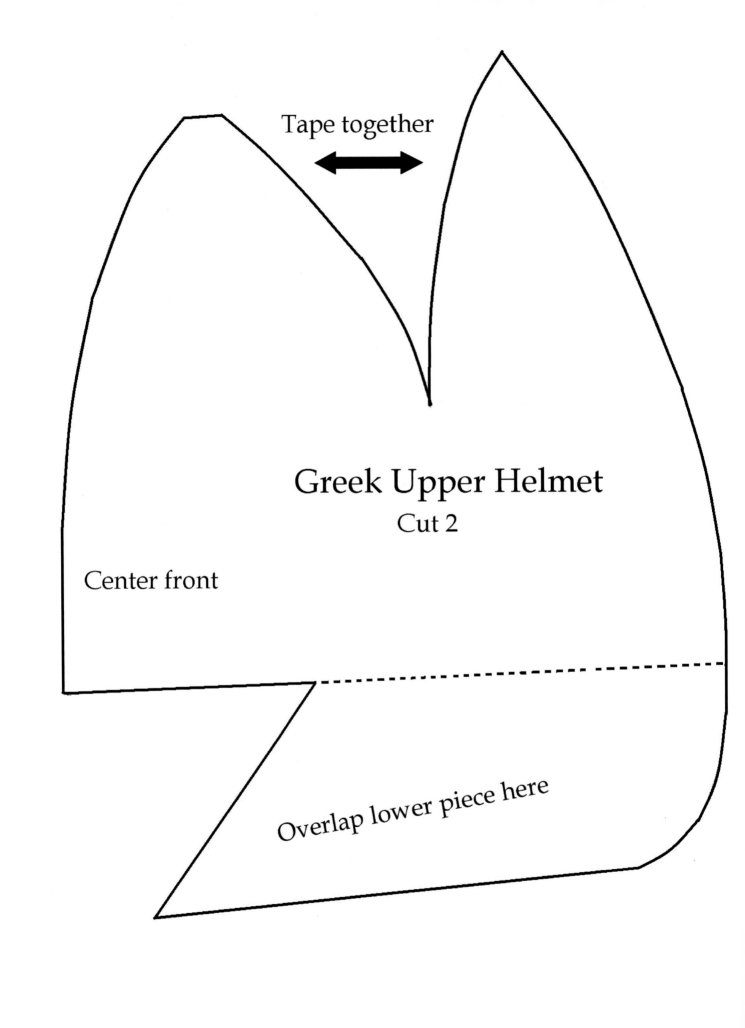

Tape together

Greek Upper Helmet
Cut 2

Center front

Overlap lower piece here

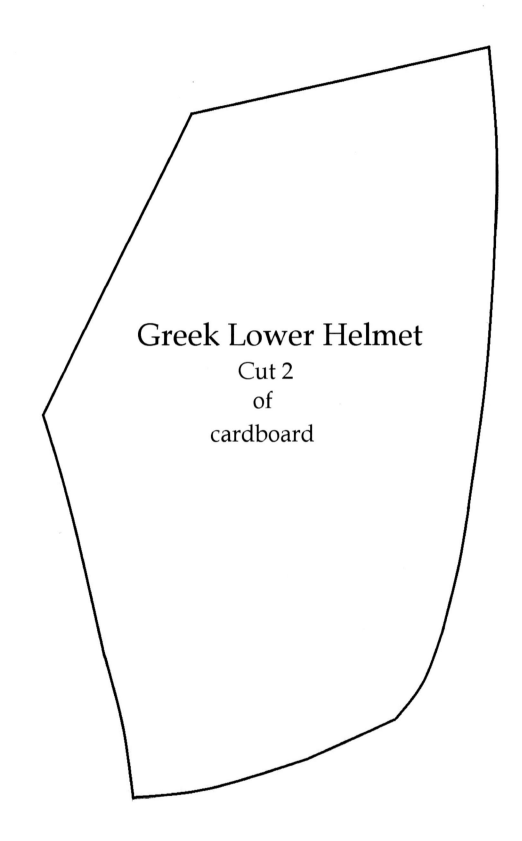

Greek Lower Helmet
Cut 2
of
cardboard

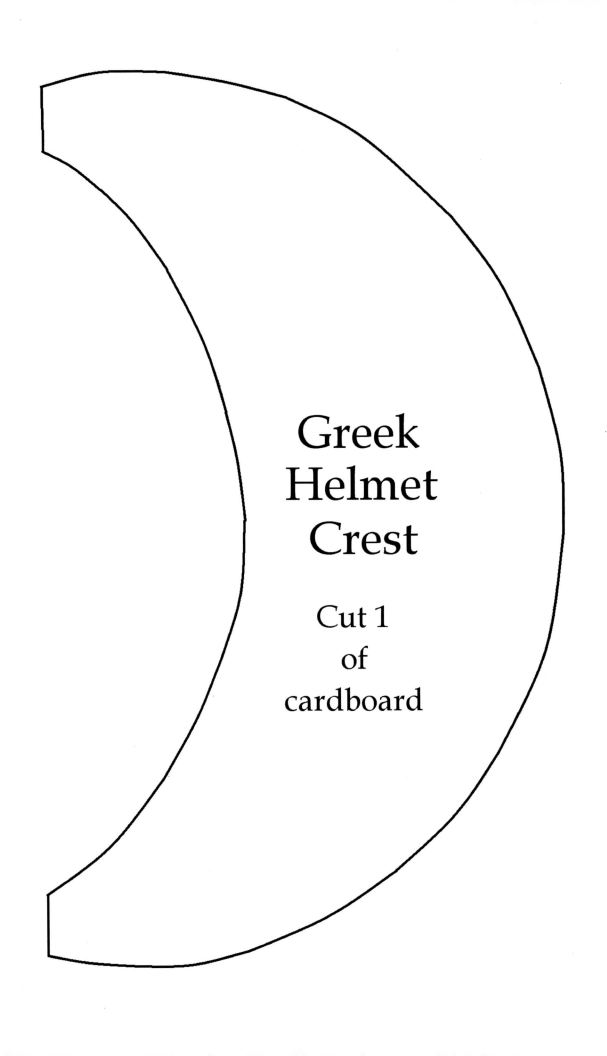

Greek
Helmet
Crest

Cut 1
of
cardboard

Cut 1
of
cardboard

Back of Helmet

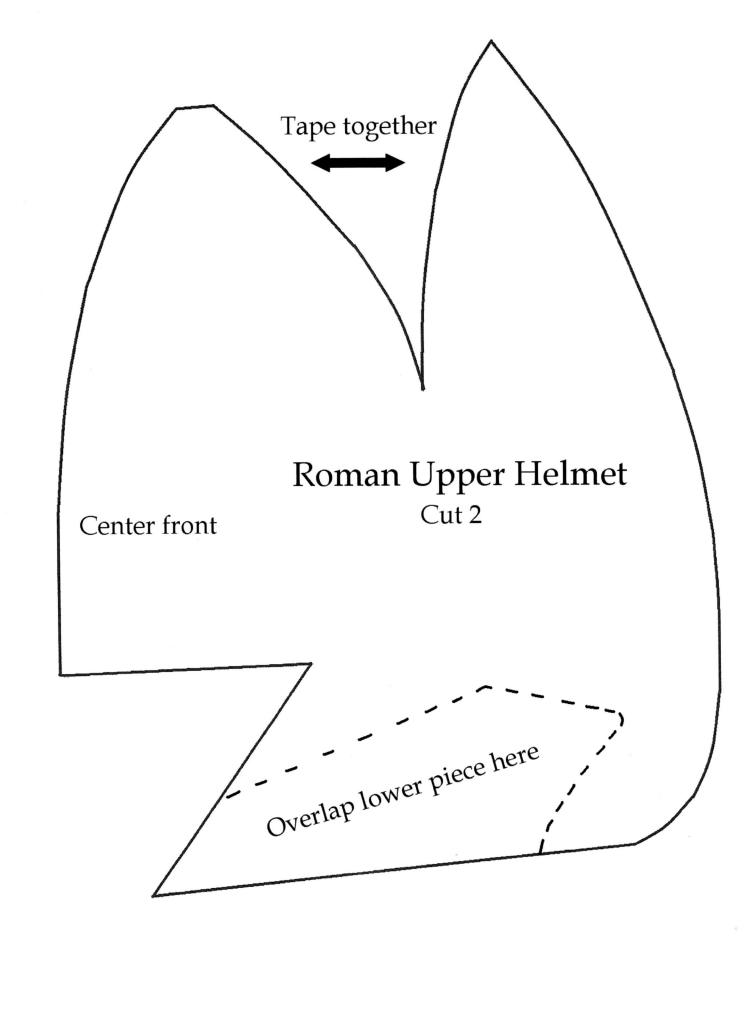

Tape together

Center front

Roman Upper Helmet

Cut 2

Overlap lower piece here

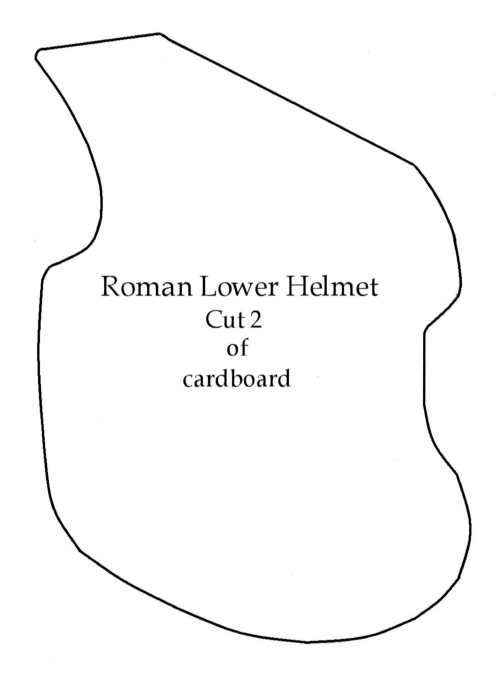

Roman Lower Helmet
Cut 2
of
cardboard

Cut 1
of
cardboard

Back of Helmet

Visit our website www.warfarebyducttape.com for more information.
Also available from Warfare by Duct Tape:

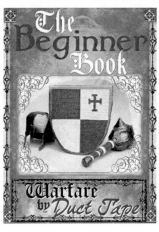

Made in the USA
San Bernardino, CA
16 May 2019